Teach Me...™
German
and
More German

by Judy Mahoney

Teach Me German and More German
Two books in one, twice the fun!
40 songs to sing and learn German

The classic coloring books *Teach Me German* and *Teach Me More German* are now combined into a new bind up edition. This new edition includes the original coloring pages from both titles with a 60 minute audio CD. *Teach Me German and More German* also features eight new pages of expanded vocabulary and activities.

Our mission at Teach Me Tapes is to enrich children through language learning. The *Teach Me...* series of books offers an engaging approach to language acquisition by using familiar children's songs and providing an audio to sing and learn. Studies show that a child's early exposure to new languages and cultures enhances learning skills and promotes a better appreciation of our multicultural world. We believe it is important for children to listen, speak, read and write the language to enhance the learning experience. What better gift to offer our youth than the tools and ideas to understand the world we live in?

The German language that children are taught in school is called "Hochdeutsch" or High German. At home, however, they may speak one of the dozens of dialects from the various regions of Germany, such as Berlinerisch, Hessisch or Bayrisch. Each dialect can sound like a different language. Not only are the vowels and consonants pronounced differently, but even entire words are different. Our products are presented in Hochdeutsch, as most Germans can speak and understand Hochdeutsch.

Today's "global children" hold tomorrow's world in their hands!

Teach Me German & More German
Bind Up Edition
Book with CD
ISBN: 978-1-59972-603-8
Library of Congress Control Number: 2009901061

Copyright © 2009 Teach Me Tapes, Inc.
6016 Blue Circle Drive
Minnetonka, MN 55343-9104
www.teachmetapes.com
1-800-456-4656

Translations are not literal.
Printed in the United States of America
10 9 8 7 6 5 4 3 2

Teach me...
GERMAN

A Musical Journey Through the Day

by
Judy Mahoney

Teach Me...™
www.teachmetapes.com

 Je öfter wir uns treffen

Je öfter wir uns treffen, uns treffen, uns treffen
Je öfter wir uns treffen, um so fröhlicher sind wir.
Deine Freunde sind meine Freunde
Und meine Freunde sind deine Freunde.
Je öfter wir uns treffen, um so fröhlicher sind wir.

Guten Tag. Ich heiße Maria.
Wie heißt du?
Das ist meine Familie.

mein Vater

meine Mutter

ich

mein Bruder

Meine Katze

Sie heißt Muschi.
Sie ist grau.

Mein Hund

Er heißt Spitz.
Er ist schwarz und weiß.

Und das ist mein Haus. Es hat ein rotes Dach
und einen Garten mit gelben Blumen.

Mein Zimmer ist blau. Es ist sieben Uhr.
Wach-auf! Wach-auf!

 Bruder Jakob

Bruder Jacob, Bruder Jacob!
Schläfst du noch? Schläfst du noch?
Hörst du nicht die Glocken, hörst du nicht die Glocken?
Bim, bem, bam! Bim, bem, bam!

Ich ziehe mich an.
Ich ziehe meine Bluse,
meine Hose und
meine Schuhe an.

Dann setze ich
meinen Hut
auf.

Ich frühstücke.
Ich esse gerne Brot
und trinke heiße
Schokolade dazu.

♪ **Kopf, Schultern, Knie und Fuß**

Kopf und Schultern, Knie und Fuß, Knie und Fuß,
Kopf und Schultern, Knie und Fuß, Knie und Fuß,
Augen, Nase, Ohren und Mund,
Kopf und Schultern, Knie und Fuß, Knie und Fuß.

Es ist schlechtes Wetter. Es regnet. Heute kann ich nicht hinaus.

 Regen, Regen, hör doch auf

Regen, Regen, hör doch auf,
Regne auf ein and 'res Haus,
Regen, Regen, hör doch auf,
Hänschen möchte spielen.

 Regenbogen

Ein lichtes Blau, ein lichtes Grün,
Farben hell am Himmel glüh'n.
Rot und gelb, oh wie schön
Bunter Regenbogen.

Das ist meine Schule. Ich sage: "Guten Morgen, Frau Schmoll." Ich lerne die Zahlen und das Alphabet.

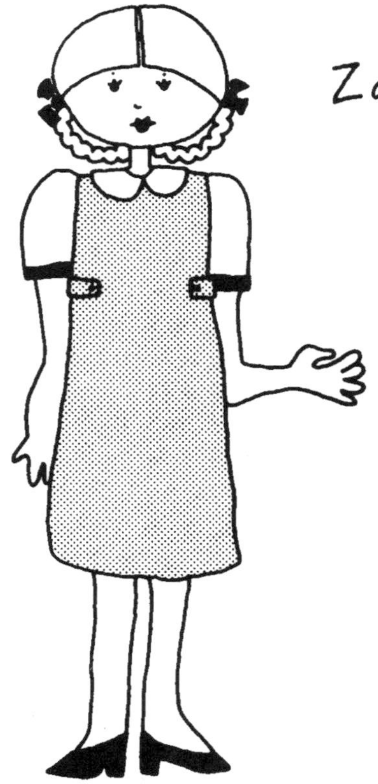

A B
C D E F G H
I J K L M N
O P Q R S T
U V W X Y Z

nun kann ich sagen um die Wett' die Buchstaben von A bis Zet.

1 2 3 4 5
6 7 8 9 10

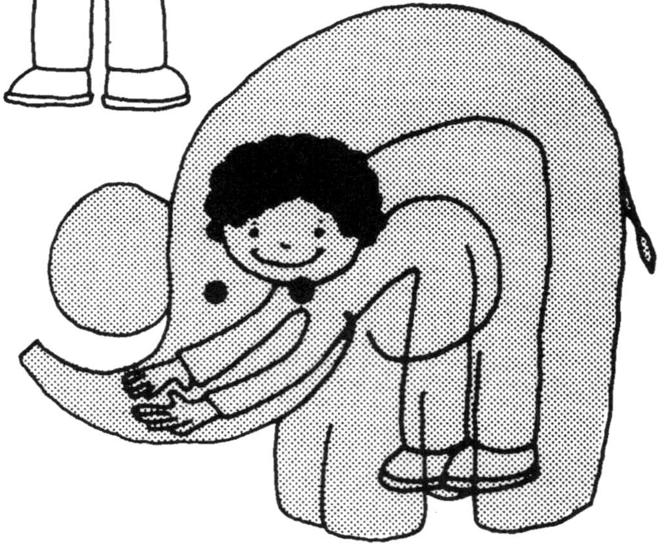

Marias süßes kleines Lamm

Marias süßes kleines Lamm,
Das hatte schneeweißes Fell.
Es lief ihr immer hinterdrein,
Lief mit auf Schritt und Tritt.

 Ein Elefant

Ein Elefant wollt' bummeln gehn,
Sich die weite Welt beseh'n.
Langsam setzt er Fuß vor Fuß,
Denn er ist kein Omnibus.
Bald ist er nicht mehr allein,
Alles trampelt hinterdrein.
Und schon singt das ganze Land.
Dieses Lied vom Elefant.

 **Brüderchen komm tanz' mit mir**

Brüderchen komm tanz' mit mir,
Beide Händchen reich' ich dir,
Einmal hin, einmal her,
Rundherum das ist nicht schwer.

Mit den Füßchen trapp, trapp, trapp,
Mit den Händchen klapp, klapp, klapp,
Einmal hin, einmal her,
Rundherum das ist nicht schwer.

Nach der Schule fahren wir mit dem Auto nach Hause.

 Die Autoräder

Die Auträder drehen sich, drehen sich, drehen sich,
Die Auträder drehen sich, durch die ganze Stadt.

Die Autohupe macht tütüt, macht tütüt, macht tütüt,
Die Autohupe macht tütüt, durch die ganze Stadt.

Die Kinder im Auto geh'n nach Haus', geh'n nach Haus', geh'n nach Haus',
Die Kinder im Auto geh'n nach Haus', durch die ganze Stadt.

 Mein liebes Kindchen

Mein liebes Kindchen schlafe ein,
Papa kauft Dir ein Vögelein.
Und wenn dein Vögelein nicht singt,
Kauft Papa einen Diamantenring.
Und wenn der Ring nicht glänzen will,
Kauft Papa Dir einen Spiegel schnell.
Und wenn der Spiegel bricht entzwei,
Bleibst Du unser liebes Kindelein.

Auf der Brück' von Avignon

Auf der Brück' von Avignon
Tanzen alle, tanzen alle,
Auf der Brück' von Avignon
Tanzen alle im Kreis herum.

 Sechs kleine Enten

Sechs kleine Enten die ich einmal sah,
Dicke, dünne und auch hübsche waren da.
Doch die eine Ente mit 'ner
Feder auf dem Rücken
Führte alle an mit ihrem quak, quak, quak,
Quak, quak, quak; quak, quak, quak.

Nach dem Mittagsschlaf gehen wir in den Park. Dort sehe ich viele Enten. Ich singe und tanze mit meinen Freunden auf der Brücke.

 Hänschen klein

Hänschen klein, ging allein, in die weite Welt hinein,
Stock und Hut steh'n ihm gut, ist gar wohlgemut,
Aber Mutter weinet sehr, hat ja nun kein Hänschen mehr,
Hänschen klein, ging allein, in die Welt hinein.

Ich habe Hunger. Es gibt Abendessen.

 Oh! Susanna

Ich komm' von Alabama, mit dem Banjo auf dem Knie,
Ich geh' nach Louisiana, wo meinen Schatz Susann ich seh'.

Oh! Susanna, ach, weine nicht um mich,
Ich komm' von Alabama, mit dem Banjo auf dem Knie.

 Siehst du die vielen Sterne steh'n

Siehst du die vielen Sterne steh'n,
Die hoch am Himmel sind zu seh'n?
Dunkel ist es in der Nacht,
Doch morgen kommt ein neuer Tag,
Ich freu' mich wenn die Sonne lacht
Und ich am Morgen froh erwach'.

 Schlaf, Kindlein, schlaf

Schlaf, Kindlein, schlaf,
Der Vater hüt' die Schaf.
Die Mutter schüttelt's Bäumelein,
Da fällt herab ein Träumelein,
Schlaf, Kindlein, schlaf!

TRANSLATIONS

PAGE 1
The More We Get Together
The more we get together, together, together,
The more we get together the happier we'll be.
For your friends are my friends
And my friends are your friends
The more we get together the happier we'll be.

PAGE 2
Hello, my name is Maria..What is your name?
Here is my family. My mother, my father,
my brother and me.

PAGE 3
My cat. His name is Muschi. He is grey.
My dog. His name is Spitz. He is black
and white. Here is my house. It has a red
roof and a garden with yellow flowers.

PAGE 4
My room is blue. It is seven o'clock.
Get up! Get up!

Are You Sleeping
Are you sleeping, are you sleeping?
Brother John, Brother John?
Morning bells are ringing
Morning bells are ringing
Ding dang dong! Ding dang dong!

PAGE 5
Today is Monday. Do you know the
days of the week? Monday, Tuesday,
Wednesday, Thursday, Friday,
Saturday, Sunday.

PAGE 6
I get dressed. I put on my shirt,
my pants, my shoes and my hat.
I eat breakfast. I like to eat bread and
drink hot chocolate with it.

PAGE 7
Head, Shoulders, Knees and Toes
Head and shoulders, knees and toes,
Knees and toes, *(repeat)*
Eyes and ears and mouth and nose.
(Repeat first line)

PAGE 8
The weather is bad. It is raining.
I cannot go for a walk today.

Rain, Rain, Go Away
Rain, rain, go away,
Come again another day,
Rain, rain, go away,
Little Johnny wants to play.

It's Raining, It's Pouring
It's raining, it's pouring
The old man is snoring
He bumped his head and went to bed
And couldn't get up in the morning.

Rainbows
Sometimes blue and sometimes green
Prettiest colors I've ever seen
Pink and purple, yellow-whee!
I love to ride those rainbows.
© Teach Me Tapes, Inc. 1985

PAGE 9
Here is my school. I say "Good
morning, teacher." I repeat my
numbers and my alphabet.

PAGE 10
Mary Had a Little Lamb
Mary had a little lamb
Its fleece was white as snow
Everywhere that Mary went
The lamb was sure to go.

One Elephant
One elephant went out to play
Upon a spider's web one day
He had such enormous fun that
He called for another elephant to come.

Brother Come and Dance with Me
Brother come and dance with me,
Take our hands and one, two, three,
Right foot first, and left foot then,
Round about and back again.
With your feet, tap, tap, tap,
With your hands, clap, clap, clap,
Right foot first, left foot then,
Round about and back again.

TRANSLATIONS

PAGE 11

After school, we drive in our car to our house.

The Wheels on the Car
The wheels on the car go 'round and 'round,
Round and 'round, 'round and 'round,
The wheels on the car go 'round and 'round
All around the town.

The horn on the car goes beep, beep, beep,
Beep, beep, beep; beep, beep, beep,
The horn on the car goes beep, beep, beep,
All around the town.

The children in the car go, "Let's have lunch,"
"Let's have lunch," "Let's have lunch,"
The children in the car go, "Let's have lunch,"
All around the town.

PAGE 12

It is lunch time. After lunch it is nap time.

Hush Little Baby
Hush little baby, don't say a word
Papa's going to buy you a mockingbird
If that mockingbird don't sing
Papa's going to buy you a diamond ring
If that diamond ring turns brass
Papa's going to buy you a looking glass
If that looking glass falls down
You'll still be the sweetest little baby in town.

PAGE 13

*After our naps, we go to the park. I see
the ducks. I sing, I dance on the bridge
with my friends.*

On the Bridge of Avignon
On the Bridge of Avignon
They're all dancing, they're all dancing
On the Bridge of Avignon
They're all dancing 'round and 'round.

Hänschen Klein
Little John went wandering into the
Wide world with his walking stick and hat.
He is happy, but his mother cries
Because she has lost her little John.
Little John went alone into the wide world.

Six Little Ducks
Six little ducks that I once knew,
Fat ones, skinny ones, fair ones too,
But the one little duck
With the feather on his back,
He led the others with his
Quack, quack, quack,
Quack, quack, quack,
Quack, quack, quack,
He led the others with his
Quack, quack, quack.

PAGE 14

I am hungry. It is dinner time.

Oh! Susanna
Well I come from Alabama
With my banjo on my knee
Going to Louisiana, my true love for to see.
Oh, Susanna, don't you cry for me
'Cause I come from Alabama
With my banjo on my knee.

PAGE 15

It's night time. Do you see the stars?

Twinkle, Twinkle
Twinkle, twinkle little star
How I wonder what you are
Up above the world so high
Like a diamond in the sky
Twinkle, twinkle little star
How I wonder what you are.

Sleep, Children, Sleep
Sleep, children, sleep,
The father guards the sheep
The mother shakes the dreamland tree,
And from it falls sweet dreams for thee,
Sleep, children, sleep.

Goodnight, My Friends, Goodnight.

*Note: All efforts have been made to include literal
translations.*

NOTES

NOTES

Teach me more... GERMAN

by
Judy Mahoney

A Musical Journey Through the Year

Learn German the fun way!

Teach Me...™
www.teachmetapes.com

Maria: Guten Tag. Ich heiße Maria. Dies ist mein Bruder. Er heißt Peter. Wir haben einen Hund. Sein Name ist Spitz. Wir haben auch eine Katze. Sie heißt Muschi. Komm mit uns auf eine Reise durch das Jahr.

Du Singst Ein Lied

Du singst ein Lied, ich sing' ein Lied, wir singen alle zusammen
...bei heit'rem oder schlechten Wetter.

Words and music by Ella Jenkins, ASCAP. Copyright 1966. Ell-Bern Publishing Co.

Peter: Es ist Frühling. Ich habe einen kleinen Blumen-
garten. Schau, hier sind meine gelben Schlüsselblumen.
Maria: Und ich pflanze Gemüsesamen. Dieses Jahr gibt es
Tomaten, Paprika und Karotten.

Alle Vögel Sind schon Da

Alle Vögel sind schon da
Alle Vögel alle
Welch' ein Singen, Musizieren
Pfeifen, Zwitschern, Tirilieren
Frühling will nun einmarschieren
Kommt mit Sang und Schalle

Kuckuck, Kuckuck

Kuckuck, Kuckuck
Ruft aus dem Wald
Lasset uns singen
Tanzen und springen
Frühling, Frühling
Wird es nun bald

APRIL

Das Zoolied

Morgen früh geht's zum Zoo mit Mutti
Zoo mit Mutti, Zoo mit Mutti
Morgen früh geht's zum Zoo mit Mutti
Wir bleiben den ganzen Tag

Wir sehen jedes Tier, Tier, Tier (Refrain)
Wie wär's mit dir, dir, dir
Du kommst mit mir, mir, mir
Wir gehen zum Zoo, hurrah

Die Affen klettern von Baum zu Baum...
Wir bleiben den ganzen Tag

Die Krokodile sind im tiefen Wasser...
Wir bleiben den ganzen Tag

Maria: Heute gehen wir in den Zoo. Wir sehen uns die Löwen, die Affen und die Giraffen an.
Peter: Mein Lieblingstier ist das Krokodil.

Ringalayo

Ringalayo, komm kleiner Affe komm
Ringalayo, komm kleiner Affe komm
Mein Affe ist flink
Und dann wieder nicht
Mein Affe kommt
Und putzt sich das Gesicht

3 DREI

Maria: Mein Geburtstag ist am 10. Mai. Ich gebe eine Party und lade alle meine Freunde ein. Meine Mutter backt mir dann einen großen leckeren Kuchen.

Peter: Also los! Spielen wir "Jürgen sagt."

Hoch Soll Sie Leben

Hoch soll sie leben
Hoch soll sie leben
Dreimal hoch!

Jürgen sagt...

Jürgen sagt:
" "Lege deine rechte Hand auf den Kopf "
" "Berühre den Boden"
" "Laufe im Kreis herum"
" "Klatsch in die Hände"
" "Sage deinen Namen"
"Lache laut"
"Das hat Jürgen aber nicht gesagt"

4 VIER

Peter: Nach dem Frühling kommt der Sommer. Unsere Familie fährt dann ans Meer.

Maria: Am Strand tragen wir unsere Badesachen, und ich habe immer mein Eimerchen und meine Schaufel dabei.

Peter: Wir bauen dann eine tolle Sandburg.

Maria: Spitz, du darfst aber die Burg nicht zerstören!

Fahr, Fahr, Fahr dein Boot

Fahr, fahr, fahr dein Boot
Langsam über'n See
Lustig, lustig, lustig, lustig
Lebewohl, ade

Ein Vogel Wollte Hochzeit Machen

Ein Vogel wollte Hochzeit machen, in dem grünen Walde
Fidiralala, fidiralala, fidiralalalala

Der Pfau mit seinem bunten Schwanz, macht mit der Braut den Ersten Tanz. Fidiralala, fidiralala, fidiralalalala

Maria: Nach dem Schwimmen machen wir ein Picknick. Wir essen Brot, Wurst und Bananen. Ich habe großen Hunger!

Peter: Igit, schau dir mal die Ameisen an!

Maria: Peter komm, wir gehen spazieren.

Sonne

Sonne, oh Sonne, Tageslicht kommt und ich will nach Haus,
Sonne...
Arbeite nachts, bis der Morgen kommt, Tageslicht...
Lad die Bananen, bis der Morgen kommt, Tageslicht...
Hey Chef, hilf mir doch mit den Bananen, Tageslicht...
Heb jetzt sechs, heb jetzt sieben, heb jetzt acht mit mir, Tageslicht...
Sonne...
Schöne, reife, gelbe Bananen, Tageslicht...

Maria: Heute besuchen wir das naturgeschichtliche Museum.
Peter: Ich gehe dort gern hin, weil es da so viele Dinosaurier gibt. Schau dir mal den Triceratop an. Er hat drei Hörner am Kopf!

Maria: Jetzt gehen wir über die Straße ins Kunstmuseum.

Peter: Ich mag den Hasen auf Dürers Bild. Er sieht so wie der Hase aus, der in unserem Garten herumhoppelt.

Maria: Schau dir mal das Bild von Van Gogh an. Die Sonnenblumen sind so schön wie die in meinem Garten.

Mädchen Steht Im Kreis

Mädchen steht im Kreis
Tra-la-la-la-la
Sie sieht so aus wie Honig
Im Bonbon, Bonbon

2.   Zeig mir doch mal was...
3.   Segel über's Meer...
4.   Tanz mir mal was vor...

Maria: Nach dem Sommer kommt der Herbst. Die Blätter färben sich rot und gold. Ich sammle gern bunte Blätter und Kastanien zum Rösten.

Kein Schöner Land in Dieser Zeit

Kein schöner Land in dieser Zeit, als hier das uns're weit und breit
Wo wir uns finden, wohl unter Linden, zur Abendszeit

Da haben wir so manche Stund', gesessen da in froher Rund'
Und taten singen, die Lieder klingen, im Talesgrund

Peter: Bevor die Schule wieder anfängt, besuchen wir Großvaters Bauernhof. Er lässt uns oft die Kühe, die Hühner und die Schweine füttern.

Maria: Großvater schert die Schafe. Später gehen wir dann alle auf eine lustige Heuwagenfahrt.

Bäh, Bäh, Schwarzes Schaf

Bäh, Bäh schwarzes Schaf, hast du etwas Woll'
Ja Herr, ja Herr, drei Säcke voll
Einen für den Meister, und einen für die Frau
Einen für den kleinen Bub, der wohnt auf der Au
Bäh, Bäh...

Onkel Oskar

Onkel Oskar hat 'ne Farm, IAIAO
Und auf der Farm da gab's 'ne Kuh, IAIAO
Da geht's Muh Muh hier, Muh Muh da
Hier ein Muh, da ein Muh, Kühe gibt es überall
Onkel Oskar hat 'ne Farm, IAIAO
...da gab's ein Huhn (Tock,Tock)...Hühner...
...da gab's 'ne Katz (Miau, Miau)...Katzen...
...da gab's ein Schaf (Bäh, Bäh)...Schafe...

Auf Opas Farm

Auf dem Weg, auf dem Weg,
Auf dem Weg zu Opas Farm
Dort auf Opas Farm
Da gibt's 'ne braune Kuh
Die Kuh hat Hunger
Und macht so: Muh Muh
....da gibt's ein rotes Huhn...

(Tock Tock)

Maria: Heute gehen wir mit unseren Eltern auf den Markt.
Die Bauern verkaufen dort viel Obst und Gemüse.
Peter: Für uns Kinder gibt es ein Karussel. Das macht
Riessenspaß!

Peter: Morgen ist St. Martinstag. Basteln wir eine Laterne!
Maria: Meine Laterne sieht aus wie ein Haus mit Fenstern.
Peters Laterne ist ganz bunt. Sie ist rot, blau, gelb und grün.
Wie schön!

Ich Geh' Mit Meiner Laterne

Ich geh mit meiner Laterne
Und meine Laterne mit mir
Am Himmel leuchten die Sterne
Und unten da leuchten wir
Mein Licht ist aus
Wir geh'n nach Haus
Labimmel, labammel, labum

Peter: Schau mal, wie der Schnee fällt! Komm wir gehen raus spielen. Wir holen einen Schlitten und fahren den Hügel runter.

Maria: Dann bauen wir einen Schneemann. Er hat Kohleaugen, eine Karotte als Nase und einen Hut auf dem Kopf. Er bekommt dann noch Muttis Schal um den Hals.

Der Schneemann

Ich habe einen Freund
Du kennst ihn ja vielleicht
Er trägt 'ne Melone
Und er ist echt gut

Er hat kohlschwarze Augen
'ne Karotte als Nase
Zwei lange dünne Arme
Und 'nen weissen Pelz

Weisst du wie er heisst
Oder möchtest du 'nen Hinweis
Im Sommer, Frühling, Herbst
Ist er nicht zu seh'n. Ja wer?

A B C, Die Katze Lief Im Schnee

A B C, die Katze lief im Schnee
Und als sie dann nach Hause kam
Da hatt' sie weisse Stiefel an
A B C die Katze lief im Schnee

Maria: Die Weihnachtsferien sind da. Wir backen Plätzchen, schmücken den Tannenbaum und singen Weihachtslieder.

Peter: Am 1. Januar fängt das neue Jahr an. Heute abend feiern wir Sylvester. Um zwölf Uhr gibt es dann ein tolles Feuerwerk!

Stille Nacht, Heilige Nacht

Stille Nacht, heilige Nacht
Alles schläft, einsam wacht
Nur das traute hochheilige Paar
Holder Knabe im lockigen Haar
Schlaf in seliger Ruh
Schlaf in seliger Ruh

Wohlauf

Wohlauf in uns're schöne Welt
Die Luft ist klar und kühl
Die Berge glüh'n wie Edelstein
Leb'wohl, auf Wiederseh'n

Maria: Im Februar feiern wir Fasching. Mir macht es Spaß die Bonbons beim Umzug zu fangen. Ich werde mein Rotkäppchenkostüm anziehen, und Peter wird ein Cowboy sein.

Peter: Nun kennen wir die Monate des Jahres. Kennst du sie auch? Januar, Februar, März, April, Mai, Juni, Juli, August, September, Oktober, November, Dezember.

Wer Soll Das Bezahlen

Wer soll das bezahlen
Wer hat soviel Geld
Wer hat soviel Pinke, Pinke
Wer hat soviel Geld

Guten Abend, Gut' Nacht

Guten Abend, gut' Nacht
Mit Rosen bedacht
Mit Näglein besteckt
Schlupf unter die Deck
Morgen früh, wenn Gott will
Wirst du wieder geweckt

TRANSLATIONS

PAGE 1
You"ll Sing a Song and I'll Sing a Song
You'll sing a song and I'll sing a song
And we'll sing a song together
You'll sing a song and I'll sing a song
In warm or wintry weather.

MARIA: Hello. My name is Maria. This is my brother Peter. We have a dog. His name is Spitz. We also have a cat. She is called Muschi. Follow us through the year.

PAGE 2 MARCH
PETER: It is spring. I have a small flower garden. Look at my yellow primroses.
MARIA: And I am planting vegetable seeds. This year we will have tomatoes, peppers and carrots.

Alle Vögel Sind Schon Da
This is a traditional German folksong about the different music birds make to announce spring.

Kuckuck, Kuckuck
This is a traditional German children's song. The cuckoo is the first bird to loudly proclaim that spring is on its way, and it encourages us to sing, dance and leap with joy.

PAGE 3 APRIL
MARIA: Today we go to the the zoo. We'll see the lions, the giraffes and the monkeys.
PETER: I like the crocodile the best.

Going to the Zoo
Mummy's taking us to the zoo tomorrow,
Zoo tomorrow, zoo tomorrow,
Mummy's taking us to the zoo tomorrow,
We can stay all day.
We're going to the zoo, zoo, zoo
How about you, you, you?
You can come too, too, too
We're going to the zoo.
2. Look at the monkeys swinging in the trees...
3. Look at the crocodiles swimming in the water...

Tingalayo
Tingalayo, come little donkey come (Refrain)
Me donkey fast, me donkey slow
Me donkey come and me donkey go. (Refrain)

PAGE 4 MAY
Hoch Soll Sie Leben
Traditional song for young children. They are usually lifted in the air three times while sitting in a small chair.
DAD: Happy birthday, Maria!
MARIA: My birthday is May 10. I'll have a party with all of my friends. Mom will bake me a big yummy cake.
PETER: Great. Let's play "Simon says":

Simon Says
Simon says ..."put your right hand on your head"
          ..."touch the ground"
          ..."walk"
          ..."clap your hands"
          ..."say your name"
"Laugh out loud." "Simon didn't say!"

PAGE 5 JUNE
PETER: After spring it is summer. Our family likes to go to the ocean.
MARIA: At the beach we wear our swimsuits and I always bring my bucket and shovel to play in the sand.
PETER: We'll build a great sandcastle!
MARIA: Spitz, you'd better not knock it down!

Row, Row, Row Your Boat
Row, row, row your boat
Gently down the stream
Merrily, merrily, merrily, merrily
Life is but a dream.

Ein Vogel Wollte Hochzeit Machen
A traditional German children's song about birds getting married in the forest.

PAGE 6 JULY
MARIA: After we swim we'll go on a picnic. We'll have bread, sausage and bananas. I am really hungry!
PETER: Yuck! Look at those ants!
MARIA: Peter come, let's go for a walk.

Day-O
Day-O, me say day-o
          Daylight come and me wan' go home
Work all night 'til the mornin' come
          Daylight ...
Stack banana 'till the mornin' come
          Daylight...
Come mister tallyman, tally me banana,
          Daylight...
Lift six hand, seven hand, eight hand bunch,
          Daylight ...
CHORUS
A beautiful bunch of ripe bananas,
          Daylight...
Lift six hand, seven hand, eight hand bunch,
          Daylight...
CHORUS

PAGE 7 AUGUST
MARIA: Today we go to the natural history museum.
PETER: I like to go there because they have dinosaurs. Look at the Triceratops! It has three horns coming out of its head.

PAGE 8
MARIA: Next we go across the street to the art gallery.
PETER: I really like the bunny in Dürer's picture. It looks like the one that hops around our lawn.
MARIA: Look at the painting by Van Gogh. The sunflowers are as pretty as the ones in my garden.

Brown Girl in the Ring
Brown girl in the ring
Tra-la-la-la-la (repeat)
She looks like a sugar
And a plum, plum, plum.
2. Show me a motion...
3. Skip across the ocean...
4. Do the locomotion...

TRANSLATIONS

PAGE 9 SEPTEMBER
MARIA: After the summer it is autumn. The leaves turn red and gold. I like to gather colorful leaves for pressing and also chestnuts for roasting.

Kein Schöner Land In Dieser Zeit
Traditional German folksong about the pleasure of sitting under a Linden tree in the evening and singing with good friends.

PAGE 10 OCTOBER
PETER: Before school begins, we'll visit Grandpa on his farm. He often lets us feed the cows, the chickens and pigs.
MARIA: Grandpa shears the sheep. Later on we will all go on a fun hayride.

Down on Grandpa's Farm
Oh we're on our way, we're on our way
On our way to grandpa's farm. (repeat)
Down on grandpa's farm there is a big brown cow (repeat)
The cow she makes a sound like this: Moo!Moo!
2. Down on grandpa's farm there is a little red hen.

Baa Baa Black Sheep
Baa baa black sheep, have you any wool
Yes Sir, yes Sir, three bags full
One for my master, and
One for the dame
One for the little boy, who lives down the lane
Baa baa black sheep, have you any wool
Yes Sir, yes Sir, three bags full.

Old MacDonald Had a Farm
Old MacDonald had a farm, E I E I O
And on his farm he had a cow, E I E I O
With a moo moo here, and a moo moo there
Here a moo, there a moo, everywhere a moo moo
Old MacDonald had a farm, E I E I O.
... had a chicken, cat, sheep.

PAGE 11
MARIA: Today we go to the market with our parents. The farmers sell their vegetables and fruit.
PETER: For us kids there is a merry-go-round. What fun!

PAGE 12 NOVEMBER
PETER: Tomorrow is St. Martin's Day. Let's make a lantern!
MARIA: My lantern looks like a house with windows in it. Peter's is really colorful. It is red, blue, yellow and green. How pretty!

Ich Geh' Mit Meiner Laterne
Traditional German children's song for St. Martin's Day. Children put candles inside the lanterns at night and walk through the neighborhood in small groups, singing songs and collecting sweets.

PAGE 13 DECEMBER
PETER: Look, snow is falling! Come, let's go outside and play. We'll take our sleds and slide down the hill.
MARIA: Then we'll build a snowman. He has charcoal eyes, a carrot nose and a hat on his head. He'll wear Mom's scarf around his neck.

Snowman Song
There is a friend of mine
You might know him too
Wears a derby hat
He's real cool.

He has coal black eyes
An orangy carrot nose
Two funny stick-like arms
And a snowy overcoat.

Have you guessed his name
Or do you need a clue?
You'll never see his face
In autumn, summer, spring. Guess who?

A B C Die Katze Lief Im Schnee
German children's song about a cat which ran out in the snow and returned with white paws.

PAGE 14 DECEMBER AND JANUARY
Happy Holidays!

Silent Night
Silent night, holy night
All is calm, all is bright
'Round yon Virgin, Mother and Child
Holy infant so tender and mild
Sleep in heavenly peace. (Refrain)

(Harp tune which follows may be used to sing along in German.)

MARIA: It's holiday time. Let's bake cookies, decorate the tree and sing Christmas songs.
PETER: January first begins the New Year. Tonight we celebrate New Year's Eve. At midnight there are great fireworks.

Wohlauf
Song about leaving to go out into the fresh and clear air where the mountains glow in the evening sun.

PAGE 15 FEBRUARY
Guten Abend, Gut' Nacht
Traditional German lullabye (Music by J. Brahms)

MARIA: In February we celebrate Mardi Gras. It's fun to catch candy at the parade. I'll wear my Little Red Riding Hood costume and Peter will be a cowboy.

Wer Soll Das Bezahlen
German Mardi Gras song. Author unknown.

PETER: Now we know the months of the year. Do you?
JANUARY, FEBRUARY, MARCH, APRIL, MAY, JUNE, JULY, AUGUST, SEPTEMBER, OCTOBER, NOVEMBER, DECEMBER.

Good-bye! See you!

Note: All efforts have been made to include literal translations.

APPENDIX:

PRONUNCIATION KEY FOR GERMAN

German pronunciation and spelling are more uniform and easier than English. Words tend to be spelled the way they are pronounced. The following are exceptions:

GERMAN LETTERS	APPROXIMATE PRONUNCIATION
v	pronounced as *f*
w	pronounced as *v*
z	pronounced as *ts*
ß	pronounced as *ss*
th	pronounced as *t*
qu	pronounced as *kw*
tion	pronounced as *tsion*
ng	pronounced as the *ng* in wi*ng*
ch	pronounced as the Scottish lo*ch*
st and sp	pronounced as in English, except at the beginning of a word, where you say *scht* and *schp*

THE GERMAN ALPHABET

GERMAN LETTER	HOW TO SAY THE LETTER	GERMAN LETTER	HOW TO SAY THE LETTER
Aa	ah	Nn	en
Bb	beh	Oo	oh
Cc	tseh	Pp	peh
Dd	deh	Qq	koo
Ee	eh	Rr	err
Ff	eff	Ss	ess
Gg	geh	Tt	teh
Hh	heh	Uu	oo
Ii	ee	Vv	fau
Jj	yott	Ww	veh
Kk	kah	Xx	iks
Ll	ell	Yy	ip-see-lawn
Mm	em	Zz	tsett

PRONUNCIATION KEY FOR GERMAN (*Continued*)

VOWELS

Note: In German, vowels are generally long when followed by *h* or by one consonant and short when followed by two or more consonants.

GERMAN LETTER	APPROXIMATE PRONUNCIATION
a	1) short like *u* in c*u*t 2) long like *a* in c*a*r
ä	1) short like *e* in l*e*t 2) long like *ai* in h*ai*r
e	1) short like *e* in l*e*t 2) long like *a* in l*a*te 3) in unstressed syllables it is generally pronounced like *er* in oth*er*
i	1) short like *i* in h*i*t 2) long like *ee* in m*ee*t
ie	- like *ee* in b*e*
o	1) short like *o* in g*o*t 2) long like *o* in n*o*te
ö	- like *ur* in f*ur* (long or short)
u	1) short like *oo* in f*oo*t 2) long like *oo* in m*oo*n
ü	- like French *u* in *u*ne; no English equivalent. Round your lips and try to say *ea* as in m*ea*n
y	- like German ü

DIPHTHONGS

ai, ay, ei, ey	- like *igh* in h*igh*
au	- like *ow* in n*ow*
äu, eu	- like *oy* in b*oy*

A B C D E F G H I J K L M N O P Q R S T U V W X Y Z

das Alphabet

 **A** der Affe	**B** die Blume	**C** das Cabrio	**D** der Dinosaurier	**E** die Eule

 **F** die Fahne

 **G** die Gitarre

 **H** der Hund

 **I** das Insekt

J die Jacke

 **K** die Katze

 **L** die Löwe

 **M** der Mund

 **N** die Nase

 **O** der Opa

 **P** der Pfefferkuchen

 **Q** das Quadrat

 **R** der Regenbogen

 **S** die Sterne

 **T** die Tasse

 **U** die Uhr

 **V** die Violine

 **W** die Welt

 **X** das Xylophon

 **Y** die Yacht

 **Z** das Zebra

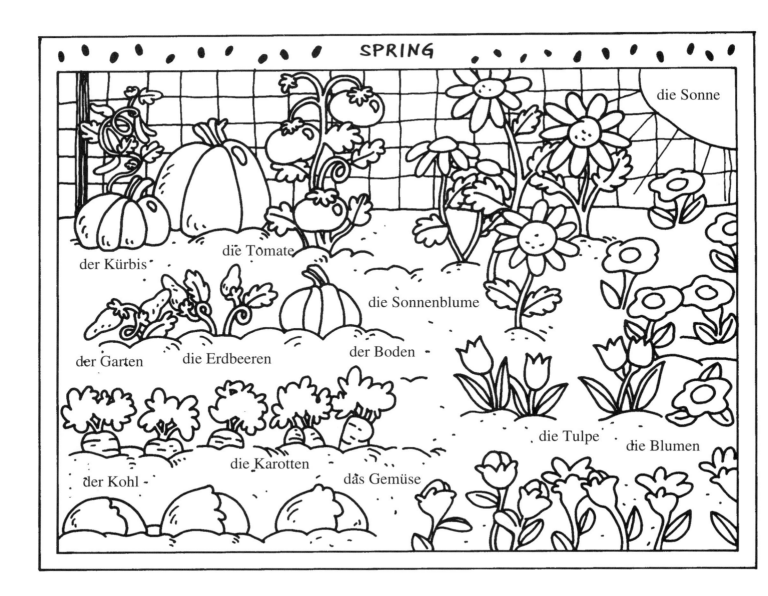

FRÜHLING
Spring Vocabulary
Find the matching words in the picture.

soil _____   garden _____

strawberries _____   tulip _____

vegetables _____   carrots _____

pumpkin _____   flowers _____

sunflower _____   cabbage _____

tomato _____   sun _____

SOMMER
Summer Vocabulary
Find the matching words in the picture.

clouds _____   cup _____

lake _____   thermos _____

beach _____   sunglasses _____

ant _____   swimsuit _____

sand _____   shirt _____

banana _____   cheese _____

sailboat _____   sandwich _____

blanket _____   shoes _____

HERBST
Autumn Vocabulary
Find the matching words in the picture.

sky _____   bird _____

leaves _____   dog _____

sweater _____   jacket _____

cat _____   pants _____

skirt _____   basket _____

nuts _____   tree _____

WINTER
Winter Vocabulary
Find the matching words in the picture.

hill _____   mitten _____

jacket _____   ice skates _____

ice _____   snow_____

snowflake_____   mouth _____

boots _____   carrot _____

hat _____   eye _____

coat _____   stick _____

sled _____   scarf _____

snowman _____

ANSWER KEY TO SEASONS VOCABULARY

FRÜHLING (Spring)

soil	der Boden	garden	der Garten
strawberries	die Erdbeeren	tulip	die Tulpe
vegetables	das Gemüse	carrots	die Karotten
pumpkin	der Kürbis	flowers	die Blumen
sunflower	die Sonnenblume	cabbage	der Kohl
tomato	die Tomate	sun	die Sonne

SOMMER (Summer)

clouds	die Wolken	cup	die Tasse
lake	der See	thermos	die Thermoskanne
beach	der Strand	sunglasses	die Sonnenbrille
ant	die Ameise	swimsuit	der Badeanzug
sand	der Sand	shirt	das Hemd
blanket	die Decke	cheese	der Käse
banana	die Banane	sandwich	das belegte Brot
sailboat	das Segelboot	shoes	die Schuhe

HERBST (Autumn)

sky	der Himmel	bird	der Vogel
leaves	die Blätter	dog	der Hund
sweater	der Pullover	jacket	die Jacke
cat	die Katze	pants	die Hose
skirt	der Rock	basket	der Korb
nuts	die Nüsse	tree	der Baum

WINTER (Winter)

hill	der Hügel	mitten	der Fäustling
jacket	die Jacke	ice skates	die Schlittschuhe
ice	das Eis	snow	der Schnee
snowflake	die Schneeflocke	mouth	der Mund
boots	der Stiefel	carrot	die Karotte
hat	der Hut	eye	das Auge
coat	der Mantel	stick	der Stock
sled	der Schlitten	scarf	der Schal
snowman	der Schneemann		